Medusa Retold

Sarah Wallis

First published December 2020 by Fly on the Wall Press
Published in the UK by
Fly on the Wall Press
56 High Lea Rd
New Mills
Derbyshire
SK22 3DP
www.flyonthewallpoetry.co.uk

ISBN: 978-1-913211-30-1

Typesetting and Cover Design by Isabelle Kenyon.
Cover Image: Unsplash, Florian Olivo.

A CIP Catalogue record for this book is available from the British
Library.

Supported using public funding by
ARTS COUNCIL
ENGLAND
LOTTERY FUNDED

i.m.
Bolthole Bill

Praise for 'Medusa Retold'

"Sarah Wallis is a very fine poet and storyteller. She deftly re-inhabits the Medusa myth, losing none of the magic and mystery and yet giving it a contemporary and affecting resonance. She salutes the ancient gods, particularly Athena but also deals with 21st century questions of identity and gender. A miniature epic full of wonderful writing."

- James Nash, poet, recent collections, "Some Things Matter: 63 Sonnets "(2012); "A Bench for Billie Holiday" (2018), both from Valley Press.

"A wild and writhing reimagination of the Medusa myth for the modern age. Mesmerising. Compelling."

- Tanya Shadrick, editor of Wild Woman Swimming.

"In this vivid retelling of the well-known Greek myth, Wallis captures Medusa's spirit of fury borne of oppression and shapes it into a contemporary story of female rage. Medusa Retold is gripping, raw and essential reading for the modern-day feminist."

- JL Corbett, editor Idle Ink

Acknowledgements

The first section (p7 to the first asterisk) was published as *Beached Lights* by The Island Review and a version of the section in italics on page 12/13 was published as *Ebb Again the Wild* by Selcouth Station.

The section on p22 to the top of p23 was printed as a stand alone poem titled *Unruhe und Fernweh* in the Oct/Nov 2020 'Stranger' issue of Finished Creatures.

A Note on the Myth of Medusa From the Author

In Greek mythology Medusa was a beautiful mortal woman that captured the eye of the sea god Poseidon. She was one of the Gorgon sisters and according to Hesiod's Theogony lived *'beyond famed Oceanus at the world's edge hard by Night'*. Poseidon defiled Medusa in the Temple of Athena and the goddess transformed Medusa into a monster, with a headful of snakes and the ability to turn a person to stone if they looked at her.

Perseus usually has the starring role, sent on a quest for Medusa's head by King Polydectes of Seriphos and expected to fail. However, with help from the gods, Perseus succeeds, and after using the head to petrify his enemies, gives the head to Athena, who wears it on her shield as protection. It is via this male and hero-fixated narrative that we come to know Medusa as a monster.

My retelling uses elements and tropes of the myth in order to tell a modern, contemporary story of a girl called Nuala. Hesiod's description and some of the art around the theme of Medusa suggested a modern day setting of a slightly run down seaside town. Swapping out the snakes for jellyfish - in Italian jellyfish are known as medusa - became a central motif, especially using the school friends as the *'medusine la compagnie'* and was a hook into the writing of the piece.

Nuala's a difficult child. Her father is gone and she is fixated with sea creatures: a puppy or kitten to cuddle is not for her! Her first memory is of protecting a jellyfish, but she's not sure if she really does remember that, or if her mother has told the story so often she thinks the memory is hers. She doesn't have sisters in this version because the story lends itself to the central character being a loner, doesn't like the things everyone else likes, she stands out, and explains why she falls headlong for someone who seems to understand her, after being so long on her own.

In this story Athena becomes Nuala's cool best friend, first crush and they spend time in a band together before the teenage duo, girl and sidekick, are ripped apart. The damage done to Nuala seems irreparable and she goes on to live an unprotected life, with a Perseus parallel in which he is most definitely not the hero but here she is almost watching herself through glass, unable to break through to save herself. Perhaps waiting for a time until she can perhaps, reunite with Athena, as in the myth when she turned from monster to protector, on the aegis of the goddess' shield.

Uncaged from the sweep of the sea
a fragile and unexpected thing is thrown
onto the beach.

                Anger at displacement
lashes out, the only thing that's free.

Investigators come to see the lights
that we might call lungs, landlubbers
and their young draw close.

                A small girl trips
and falls, giving her armpit to cradle

a jellyfish, both gasping on the sand.
Torchlight and silence fall on the wobbled
mass of tangled girl

                and tentacle; they
breathe the shivered tide.

To revenge themselves and show the girl
what protection of the pack meant, they cut
the jellyfish, which had acted on its nature

                as each took part in theirs,
but for all the puzzled science they only found
a transparent,
dying on the beach and they couldn't find the lights.

                        *

The girl, Nuala, pulls to her feet and
drags in the sand, her mother would drag
her, furious, by her hair if there weren't so many

snake eyes watching, smothering giggles,
pointing and judging, she is embarrassed,
has never known how

to handle her headstrong girl with her outsize
feelings for the sea and her cool-eyed creatures,
not for her the domestic comfort of a cat

or a charming puppy to cuddle, but cold-blooded
reptiles kept in temperate tanks, staring inviolate
all hooded eyes and hisses and ululating tongues

like her, they are creaturely, primal
with desperate, cold, strange furies, burning
within and waiting to burst forth

and her mother knows things will just get
harder, there's no one at home to lay down
the law and she's just too tired to do it anymore,

our girl Nuala, she's growing up spiky,
does things her own way and won't be told.
The girl who found a jellyfish lying on the sand

and protected it with her own brand of loyalty
cries fealty to the sea, finds her own way to be creaturely
stands alone, with her snakes and iguanas,

salamanders and newts, reptiles of all stripes,
won't have parties, won't make friends, her mum
doesn't know the half of what goes on,

closes her eyes to it, hopes and prays
one day, her straying daughter will come back to her side.

*

She's older now, a punk princess, in a sea-green
tutu and purple glitter Doc Martens stomping across

the rocks in hobnailed fury at some schoolyard
injustice, a roaring girl, shouting, singing out
loud, screaming appropriated pain
sure, she's had it rough, so what, plenty have it worse
but she's never known how to keep quiet, how to play
well with others, her sense of fair play and natural justice
a lonesome mystery to the other girls and boys,

goading this latchkey kid, whose mum has to work
two jobs to keep body and soul together, the father long gone,
Italian itinerant, idealist and dreamer,

Alessandro for the summer, left her mother, Cathleen,
holding the baby and Cathleen is still holding on,
calming her rages, holding back her hair as she throws up again

after nightclubs and pubs and all the growing up stages.

*

So she's seventeen at last, at one with the sea
her sea-caged voice letting loose in a band
(but they won't let her sing)

employed as a dancer, soon discovers a talent
for mad-eyed drumming skillz, sticks and dreads
flying out her head, beating out a rhythm

keeping them in time, *two three four*

band mate Athena is well impressed with her,
signing out - singer songwriter and lead on guitar
she's never let anyone else in or let them go so far,
the rhythm leads them on, they lose themselves in it...
But Athena has a problem, that no one will
acknowledge, strums a riff or two, stoned by 2 pm,
and the band's got no further than her Dad's old garage
Nuala takes charge, kicks out all the rest

their sound is changing, ranging further, they get
some bookings and are gonna be the best
do the birthdays of all her schoolmates,
so they want to be friends now when they see her up

on stage and have to admit, *oh yeah, she's cool now,*

Athena laughs with her, is completely on her side
calls them the *medusine la compagnie* –
the company of jellyfish, it takes her back to the scene

on the sand, on the beach, all reconstructed memory
Cathleen has told the story so many times, the girl
and the jellyfish... the crowd of one mind.

But it's alluring to be the cool one, the one
they all want to be, the boys come on strong
and so do the girls, she's got big life choices now

does she want to be one of them, or work on revenge?

There's Rolo & Roni, Goth twins in androgyny
she finds so intriguing, Jemma & Dolores,
the alpha girls she has so firmly set against,

the lone outsider suddenly become interesting
to the whole cast of bored English seaside town youth,
Jackson, Penny, Sadie, Rick, April, and Lyssa…

Oh, Lyssa, the ex, the stony-eyed minx, that can still flip her
heart, she's been at odds with them for years, temperamentally
culturally, politically, sexually, and now they find her

interesting again, she wishes she could think straight
but her internal song just wants Lyssa, Lyssa, Lyssa…

*

La tendresse / for the old
lie / of affection / between us / and dressed

in your mother of pearl / for the eccentric
caught in the rain, for friendship / once held tight,
for / the woman /

for the mother of pearl /
for the woman / on her way
to the seaside and dressed in her mother's
pearls / who insists on dancing the beach
/ in a long
ball-gown, / and barefoot,

but / otherwise utterly unsuited to drag
through the surf / in salted teal taffeta / mermaidic silk wrap

bladderwracked, /
la tendresse for the footprints / dressed
in loose ropes and losing / mother / of pearl

creeping over broken clamshell, / fish guts
and old abandoned barbeque / filthy sanded
lucre of mussel instep / she's lost her mother,
of pearl / barbs

of jelly and odd squares of cuttle, / crying
with laughter as a white wave knocks her down / to sit

in the sharp sand, building / lost castles, the future sobs,
away / awhile, searching / searching out lost mother
of pearl / the veiled glint of bright dream / 'til shipwreck
come / again, and again, and ebb again the wild

*

The school are on a scuba trip and the band
is going too, Nuala's got Athena as a partner,
the only one she'd trust to go down to the ocean bed.

They listen to the coach, assembled in their gear,
no one is playing up, they understand and have things clear
Nuala and Athena are the first to go under

the experienced divers, the others watch them carefully
and take their cue, then it's off into the blue, cold
aquarium to see what they can see, now, only half an hour

from tragedy. It's Athena that gets into difficulty
and pulls on the rope, something's wrong with her air supply
and she's starting to choke, panic, kicks for the surface,

Nuala's got her ankle caught in a rocky crevice,
cuts the line and shoots up too fast, can't shout out
in her facemask, she knows it's a risk, going up too quick

and feels a rupture in her ear

a howl of pain escapes from her and her facemask disappears,

the Goth twins have seen what's going down, one of them
lights a flare, the others have forgotten about, the red light
draws them to the surface slowly, save Athena,

who's thrashing like a fish caught in a net, blue lights flash
and Athena is hauled out, and off to hospital, she's got the bends
and Nuala's got a perforated eardrum, the sound's punched out.

At the hospital there's no news and Cathleen
is praying for the fate of her child's best and only
friend –

she doesn't know what she would do
and what would she do without her best mate.

The hours go by and there's no word,
Nuala's pacing the ward and wobbly, no balance with one
eardrum gone, the hate in her heart turning her to stone,

and when they give her the news, the very worst news
she becomes what she always had the potential to become
the Godhead, the steely-eyed Gorgon, the Medusa re-born.

*

They say I'm angry like I haven't got

the right / like the snakes

in my head sound too loud, and too bright, /   they are

drumming out the dead and then they're drumming

out the light /

fury makes blood patterns shooting thoughts and sights

of course I'm bloody angry, but that's not enough, not nearly

enough

I am incandescent with rage

and I can't understand why they don't think that's

all right, / that maybe it's just a phase, / a stage

of growing up and getting on and accepting things

have / happened /

that weren't meant to be but just are… / sorry

not bloody sorry / I can't do that, I can't accept

the bar being so low / that we have to step

over it, not limbo

under / I'm sorry you can't accept my anger

and I'm sorry that my best friend / is dead, /

it could have been avoided,

it should have been avoided / it would have been

avoided if things had been / different, /

different how, different who, different

when, / all of this is just

over and over again, I can't cry any more

I can only rage, it's all that I've got left

and I wish that you could / see this, see how I'm bereft.

*

Nuala's up in arms but she just can't cry, and she's
angry now, more than she's ever been, for Athena, now,
now, now, she's going to get mean

going to be more herself than she has ever been and this town
is going to see something they've never seen, she shakes out
her salt long braids,

saturated with the sun god's fire, let the bright sparks
of jelly stings crackle on her skin, the one with the welts
and purple rivulets, curating the skin she's been living in,

rippling across her shoulders, like a snake about to shed,
no one will cross her now, no one shakes their head
as they look at her wield the maggoty hate in her heart

how it takes hold, makes her lose her reason, aim high
and bold, snaking lines and curves of movement,
dancing thoughts of revenge spinning spiders in her head.

The world is more whooshy / and watery / than it was,

ears singing / like a seashell / with damped down / noise

losing balance to tinnitus, / helps be /

in my own dark world, / more to worry about than

making friends, making reparations, making nice,

when no one can look, / she / who was one of two, / they /

see her coming in windows, in mirrors, they block / her gaze

and turn away, / none can speak / to her while she wears

this cloak / of tragedy,

wrong place, wrong / time,

her grief is overwhelming, / her silence

immense

The twins turn their backs / and stack books,

the alpha girls / can find nothing to say, or giggle
about, / the boys

stare at the floor

no girl looks directly at her / as if they might turn

to stone, /
even Lyssa, / Lyssa

who knows her best, has nothing to say, / no comfort to give,

no one shares this grief, / they did not know Athena, or want to,

it's something like survivor guilt, labelled and writ large

It's All Nuala's Fault.

Medusine la Compagnie they always were and shall / remain.

She won't look to Lyssa / again /

she who has her heart still, / though she could

wish it wasn't so.

Wishes she could just
let go. / But no / no/ no /

Nuala stands on the hill, looks out at the town, watching
through her fingers like when she was a girl
peeping through the arms of the statuary, the angels winged
and lost, elaborate headstones,

entwined arms of godmothers past, favoured hounds
and horses, war sprites and words from the bible

she and Athena used to come here to drink cider on the lots,
they didn't care if it was disrespectful

these had their time over and now it was their chance

she thinks of her friend now and the tears roll down

missing her so much she can't sing or even speak
but she's banned from the funeral and saying her last goodbyes

her mother had to tell her, and Cathleen, she thinks it was
the hardest blow, something so mean, her girl is suffering too…
so she runs up the hill and hides her tears among the statues
thinks she'd like to sort a Viking funeral

a big wooden boat, set on fire and sent out on the water,
a dignified funeral pyre, thinks to herself

a boat is a harness, a link

between us, and the all nature's
watery slink. An unknowable force,
ever movable body, with only
the moon to tame and betide her,
glinting at secrets and ever above her.

A boat is a crib, or a coffin

launched in hope or lament, Viking
or cargo, afire or asleep,
she whistles the wind to rock out
the tides, all general tilt, and lift,
show, and recover.

A boat is a restless creature,

full of breath and desire, a sway
dance breeze of a red sail sliding,
lifted up like hands to their prayers
and a belief in higher powers,
life entrusted to board and to flap,

a boat is chasing the horizon, all hours,

superstition, her constant, blue-lined
keel and a carefree calling, born
into a cool sea breeze unruhe
und fernweh, heeds a call
to adventure, canary yellow deck

and a boat sails on, the blue ocean slaps.

*

And now there's a man thinks he knows me,
wants what's in my head, I can't think I believe him
think it's my body he wants instead

but I'm a blur of movement and so is he
can't control his wanting and at least
he wants me
at least,
I'm good for something and it shuts out
the snaking voices in my head,
for a while, I can think of something else

than Athena's vivid smile, he says he's going
to take care of me and sometimes I wish he would
I've dropped out of school again just because I could

Mum wasn't happy but Mum doesn't get a say
I'm old enough now to make my own way and my man
lets me stay at his, home away from home

Mum can say she's disappointed, didn't work
all those hours so I can be a teenage mum
stats on the side, she's spouting them in hate

I can't stay to listen, and go or I'll be late
oh he's got a temper yeah, so what, it's true…
at least he doesn't scare me or beat me black and blue.

But I see a warning face staring in the mirror
and have to cover up the truth, can't stand her staring
back at me with her snake tattoo rippling into muscle

all grainy green and blue, and I wonder where she went
that girl I used to know, cut off in her prime, says Cathleen,
and I don't know what to do
a boy has turned her head and he's using her for sure
and I can't see the future standing on the shore but it looks
bleak for me and mine and I want to wake her up,

look at your life and mine before she's suddenly
turned forty and regrets what's done is done, Athena
wouldn't want this for you and past love is gone

you should learn to honour her and get some self-respect
leave this man who's no good for you and take time to reflect
get back into college and start again...

of course they'll take you back
this time is so important and you don't get it back
you don't get it back.

When I told him what was going down, he had
a mental break, started cutting on me and my braids
gone to snakes

then I really was afraid and I thought he would end me there

looking in the kitchen and kneeling on the stair, thought
I saw for a moment, in my window reflection: Athena
stood there, waiting in her chamber for someone to do her hair

and then there was a blinding mirror flash —

some, too many, somethings...
said aloud in anger, in all the unlacing, brutal silences...

until what was bruising us and our lives together
was all too much intensity, battling heads,

crossing swords, with each other's sanctity

one of us had to move or scream aloud the act

and I knew I had to be the one, it was either him or me

it seemed such a mean, low, trick I couldn't believe it real,

I had to move and be so quick but he was faster still

and then it was he broke my neck upon the windowsill.

*

I hope I haunt him all his days with the trophy of my head
redeemer of his dreams and the harbinger of dread
no mirror to look around or reflect the aegis on his shield

I was made for more than this,
so much more than this,
and only to Athena will I bend and yield.

Author Biography

Sarah Wallis is a poet & playwright based in Scotland, relocated from Yorkshire in 2019. She has an MA in Creative Writing from UEA and an Mphil in Playwriting from Birmingham University. Theatrical residencies include Leeds Playhouse and Harrogate Theatre, which supported her play The Rain King and development of Laridae. This play, of which three versions can be programmed, in English, in British Sign Language and integrated, with eight performers, has seen further support from Southwark Playhouse and is planning a tour for when theatres reopen. Her poetry has been included in The Yorkshire Poetry Anthology, Best New British Poets 2018 and 2019/20 and the Ways to Peace anthology marking the UN Day of Peace celebrations 2019, see sarahwallis.net

About Fly on the Wall Press

A publisher with a conscience.
Publishing high quality anthologies on pressing issues,
chapbooks and poetry products, from exceptional poets around
the globe. Founded in 2018 by founding editor, Isabelle Kenyon.

Other publications:
Please Hear What I'm Not Saying
(February 2018. Anthology, profits to Mind.)
Persona Non Grata
(October 2018. Anthology, profits to Shelter and Crisis Aid UK.)
Bad Mommy / Stay Mommy by Elisabeth Horan
The Woman With An Owl Tattoo by Anne Walsh Donnelly
the sea refuses no river by Bethany Rivers
White Light White Peak by Simon Corble
Second Life by Karl Tearney
The Dogs of Humanity by Colin Dardis
Planet in Peril
(September 2019. Anthology, profits to WWF and The Climate
Coalition.)
Small Press Publishing: The Dos and Don'ts by Isabelle Kenyon
Alcoholic Betty by Elisabeth Horan
Awakening by Sam Love
Grenade Genie by Tom McColl
House of Weeds by Amy Kean and Jack Wallington
No Home In This World by Kevin Crowe
The Goddess of Macau by Graeme Hall

Social Media:
@fly_press (Twitter)
@flyonthewall_poetry (Instagram)
@flyonthewallpoetry (Facebook)
www.flyonthewallpoetry.co.uk